To all those who still dream, explore and question, and to my loving family, who permits me to still be disruptive.

—David

For the Artists that don't give up, and for my family who doesn't let me quit.

—Alex

It was a beautiful, sunny morning for running — jumping and most importantly — kicking.
Pinto Bean wasn't like the race horses who were staying comfortable out of the sun in their stall.
Instead, PB preferred to pretend he was a bronco and truly loved to kick up his hindquarters.

"Whoo-Hooo!"

PB shouted as he bucked around the pasture.

"I'm a Wild Bucking Bronco,
Yee-Haw!"

Each race horse had a very strong opinion about P.B.'s behavior.

"That boy is one loose horse, such a surplus of energy."

"Look at him jumping about making a fool of himself."

"Yes sir, PB needs to go to school and learn some manners, how to act like a race horse, I'd say!"

"PB," Jay explained, "the racing fellas believe you need to be in — S-C-H-O-O-L!"

"School? Is school anything like a rodeo?
I bet there are cowboys and things to jump over and even big blue barrels to race around!"

Jay was not entirely sure what "SCHOOL" was about either,
"I believe this is where children learn how to explore,
how to be creative and innovative,
or perhaps even a champion rodeo bronco."

"S-C-H-O-O-L" just so happened to be the little red building just beyond the pasture fence.
The two friends waited for the children to leave — took a peak inside — and discovered a way to

SQUEEZE and WIGGLE

into the spaces where the children sat.

"QUAAAAACK!

I CAN'T SEE ANYTHING!" Jay honked.

PB wasn't happy either, his hind legs were jammed up under the desk so tight that he was making it float in the air like a flying carpet.

"This chair is harder than a log," PB brayed. "I can't sit on a log. I need to be up and running about! This place does not fit me!"

"I got an idea!" Jay exclaimed.
"There is a place where I learned to paddle—where the school of fish meet to discuss important things like comfort and temperature. Perhaps they know a thing or two about space."
PB chimed in, "Sounds perfect!"

"Whoa! I'm not so sure about this!" snorted PB.
"It's wet and cold and I can't hear a word the fish are saying."
"Sure... Gurgle!... you can... Burble! Gurgle!... You just need to stick your head in," bubbled Jay.

PB had no idea that they had just disrupted an important lesson. As he placed his head near the water's surface, PB heard the muffled voice of Mr. Angler the head fish master. "You know — Mr. PB", Mr. Angler croaked!
"This pond is no place for creatures that do not have scales or gills or even feathers.
Why don't you try the rabbit warren just through those cat tails.
I hear Mrs. Rabbit does a bit of homeschooling."

"Howdy Mrs. Rabbit! We're looking for a place where I can learn to become a bronco."
"Oh! Oh! Dear," Mrs. Rabbit stuttered, "Oh, da-da-dear, you can't be in here, you most certainly will not fit. Springing about will disrupt the children."

"Oh dear, this colony must learn about the dangers of the farmer and ways to hide. This is no place for a horse!"
Mrs. Rabbit suggested visiting the school of crows as they know a lot about Hopping and Bouncing on the—

Telephone Lines!

"You are too heavy!", Jay explained, "You are way too big to be balancing on the wire with the birds of a feather! You have no wings! This is not safe! You must come down right away to find a different place."

The crows agreed, "CAW—CAW—CAW—ANYWHERE BUT HERE!"
One of the angered crows thought he would trick PB and Jay and flapped about the B-School within a very old tree. PB thought "B" stood for bronco and the two friends scampered off to find the tree.

Buzzzzzzz!

Mzz. Bumble, the Uni-versa-B professor, was right in the middle of her pollination discussion when PB and Jay popped in. PB pondered, "I wonder if that crow meant B-E-E-E-E-E school?"

"You betcha!" Confirmed Jay,
"Buzzing and honey has nothing to do with jumping and running
other than to exit this place."
 And at the very moment when PB and Jay dropped out of the tree,
a disorderly traffic jam was in the midst of inching by.

Ba-Ba-Baaaaaa! Was the sound heard upon impact.

"Jay, where are you?" Neighed PB, as he popped up within the fluff of a mobile cotton ball.

"Here I am," responded Jay, sticking his head out from the side of a sheep aimlessly moving forward.

"This school is very crowded and restless," reported PB.
"There are too many obstacles for safe landings! This place does not fit me!"
As the conveyor of sheep moved across the field, PB saw what he thought was the perfect place.

"This is it! This is the place!" PB kicked up his heels in joy.
"There is plenty of space to run and jump."
To the friend's surprise, they paraded smack into a discussion about ice cream.

The young cows giggled at PB's display wishing to join him.
However, the older bovine would have none of this disturbance in the herd.

"If you want to kick up a storm, this is not the place." The large bull suggested,
"Go check out the recycling school near the hen house where there is plenty of energy."

Nom Nom Nom! The recycling lessons appeared to be progressing well with the kids up on the roof. However, after the event with the crows, PB had no interest in high places.

Instead, he wedged the front his body up into the chicken coop to see what all the loud cackling was about, only to find Ms. Henrietta in the core of a math lesson. "Hmm, I wonder—"

"Cock-a-doodle-doo!"

Pinto Bean had been unaware of the rooster closely guarding the hen house entry and was absolutely startled!

The roosters squawk caused PB to crash right through the back of the classroom and—

Straight into...

Ms. Pearl's etiquette class!

SPLASH!

Mud flew EVERYWHERE
disrupting the piglets lesson on table manners.

Wheee! One of the younger piglets was thrilled about the abrupt intrusion.

"Look at me, I'm a rowboat!" exclaimed the joyful student in the middle of his backstroke.

Discouraged that he would never find a place to fit him best, PB cleaned himself off and followed Scout, the farmer's dog, to the main house.

The two friends peered through the farmhouse window.

Searching — Wondering — Questioning.

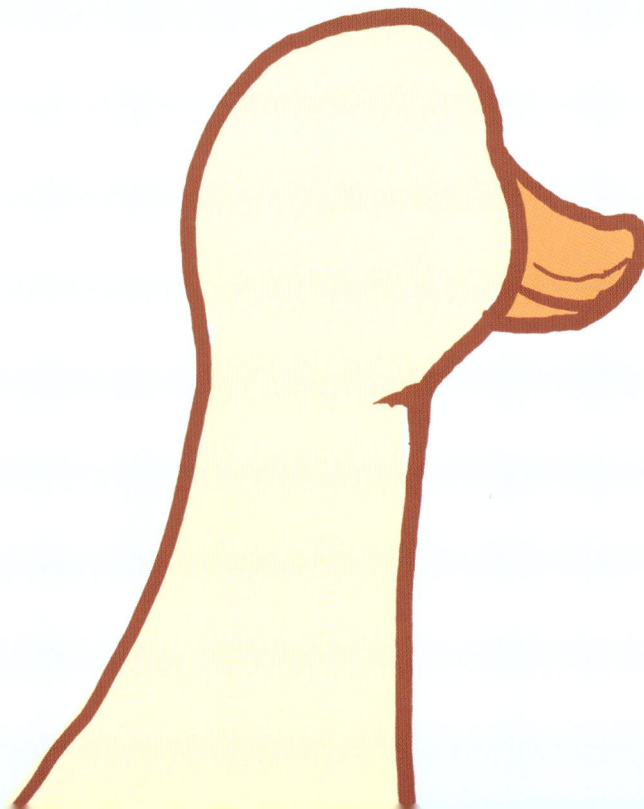

Could Scout possibly help PB find the right fit?

"I think I know what you are looking for," Scout woofed.

"An amazing learning environment exists where all types of learners can truly feel comfortable in their own skin.

Let me take you there."

The new friends flew—

and they galloped—

and they sprinted—

to this special new place

Through the opening of the barn, the friends could immediately see that there was a wide variety of space.

Places to Soar and to Sit—

Areas to Climb and to Rest—

and of course,

Room to Jump and to Kick.